Dragons
of Chinese Mythology

BY SAMANTHA S. BELL

CONTENT CONSULTANT
GANG LIU, PhD
ASSOCIATE TEACHING PROFESSOR
CARNEGIE MELLON UNIVERSITY

Kids Core

An Imprint of Abdo Publishing
abdobooks.com

abdobooks.com

Published by Abdo Publishing, a division of ABDO, PO Box 398166, Minneapolis, Minnesota 55439. Copyright © 2023 by Abdo Consulting Group, Inc. International copyrights reserved in all countries. No part of this book may be reproduced in any form without written permission from the publisher. Kids Core™ is a trademark and logo of Abdo Publishing.

Printed in the United States of America, North Mankato, Minnesota.
102022
012023

THIS BOOK CONTAINS RECYCLED MATERIALS

Cover Photo: iStockphoto
Interior Photos: Shutterstock Images, 4–5, 24, 28 (bottom), 29 (bottom); Walter Bibikow/Age Fotostock/SuperStock, 6; Christopher Brewer/Shutterstock Images, 8; Werner Forman/Universal Images Group/Getty Images, 9; Sepia Times/Universal Images Group/Getty Images, 10, 18; iStockphoto, 12–13, 29 (top); Prachaya Roekdeethaweesab/Shutterstock Images, 15; Jenny Reynish/Ikon-New Paradigm Images/SuperStock, 16, 28 (top); Liang Xiaopeng/Xinhua News Agency/Getty Images, 20–21; Zhou Hongfeng/Visual China Group/Getty Images, 22; Wang Jilin/Visual China Group/Getty Images, 25; Steve Andrew Vidler/Prisma/SuperStock, 26

Editor: Ann Schwab
Series Design: Ryan Gale

Library of Congress Control Number: 2022940673

Publisher's Cataloging-in-Publication Data

Names: Bell, Samantha S., author.
Title: Dragons of Chinese Mythology / by Samantha S. Bell
Description: Minneapolis, Minnesota: Abdo Publishing, 2023 | Series: Chinese Mythology | Includes online resources and index.
Identifiers: ISBN 9781532199936 (lib. bdg.) | ISBN 9781098275136 (ebook)
Subjects: LCSH: Dragons--Juvenile literature. | Animals, Mythical--Juvenile literature. | Mythology, Chinese--Juvenile literature.
Classification: DDC 299.51--dc23

CONTENTS

Dragons are one of the
most powerful symbols of
Chinese culture.

4

CHAPTER 1

The Red Pearl

A mother and her son lived in a village near the Yangtze River in China. They were very poor and had little food. Every day, the son went to the river to cut some grasses for them to eat. One day, the grasses he cut tasted very good.

In Chinese art, dragons are shown chasing pearls to symbolize their pursuit of wisdom.

The next day, he went back to the same place to cut more. He cut more the day after that. But the patch of grass did not get any smaller.

Then the boy found a red pearl in the patch of grass. He took it home to show his mother. They left it in the basket with a bit of grass. The next morning, the basket was filled with grass. The boy's mother put the pearl in a rice jar. The next morning, the jar was full of rice.

Chasing a Treasure

In paintings and other artwork, Chinese dragons are often shown playing with pearls. Sometimes they chase the pearls. Other times they hold pearls in their mouths or claws. Pearls represent wisdom. Some people believe they bring luck and prosperity.

To the Chinese people, dragons represent power, strength, and good luck.

Soon, neighbors heard about the pearl and wanted to see it. The boy decided to take the pearl back to the river. But he accidentally swallowed it. Suddenly, he was very thirsty. He drank and drank water from the river. Finally, he raised his head to look at his mother. His head had become the head of a dragon. She watched as his body grew longer until he had completely turned into a dragon. Then he jumped into the water, shaking his head to say goodbye.

Dragons have long been popular figures in other East Asian countries too, as shown in this Japanese illustration from the 1800s.

Helpful, Not Harmful

This story is called a myth. Chinese myths are a collection of folktales, religious traditions, and historical stories. Some describe how the world was created. Others are about Chinese culture or government. Some myths have been passed down for thousands of years.

Dragons play important roles in Chinese myths. Chinese dragons were not evil monsters like many of the dragons in the West. Instead, dragons helped people. Some lived in lakes and rivers and brought rain. Others lived in the heavens and protected the villages.

Explore Online

Read the story on the website below. Compare it with the story in this chapter. How is it different? How is it similar?

The Dragon's Pearl

abdocorelibrary.com/dragons-of -chinese-mythology

Dragons in Chinese myths
had a unique mix of body
parts from different creatures.

CHAPTER 2

Power of the Dragon

In Chinese myths, the dragon looked like it had body parts from nine different creatures. It had the head of a camel, horns of a deer, and ears of a bull. The eyes were like those of a demon. It had a long, thin neck like a snake and the belly of a clam.

The body was covered in scales like a fish. Its feet had the paws of a tiger with claws like an eagle. In some Chinese myths, all the other animals came from the dragon.

Chinese dragons were powerful creatures. They could control the water in lakes, seas, and rivers. They could fly, even if they usually did not have wings. From the sky, dragons could control the weather. In some stories, dragons created the clouds with their breath.

One famous dragon was called Yinglong. Yinglong controlled the rain. In some myths, he joined certain rulers in battle. He could store up the water and then send so much rain that it flooded the enemy's land.

The Dragon's Body

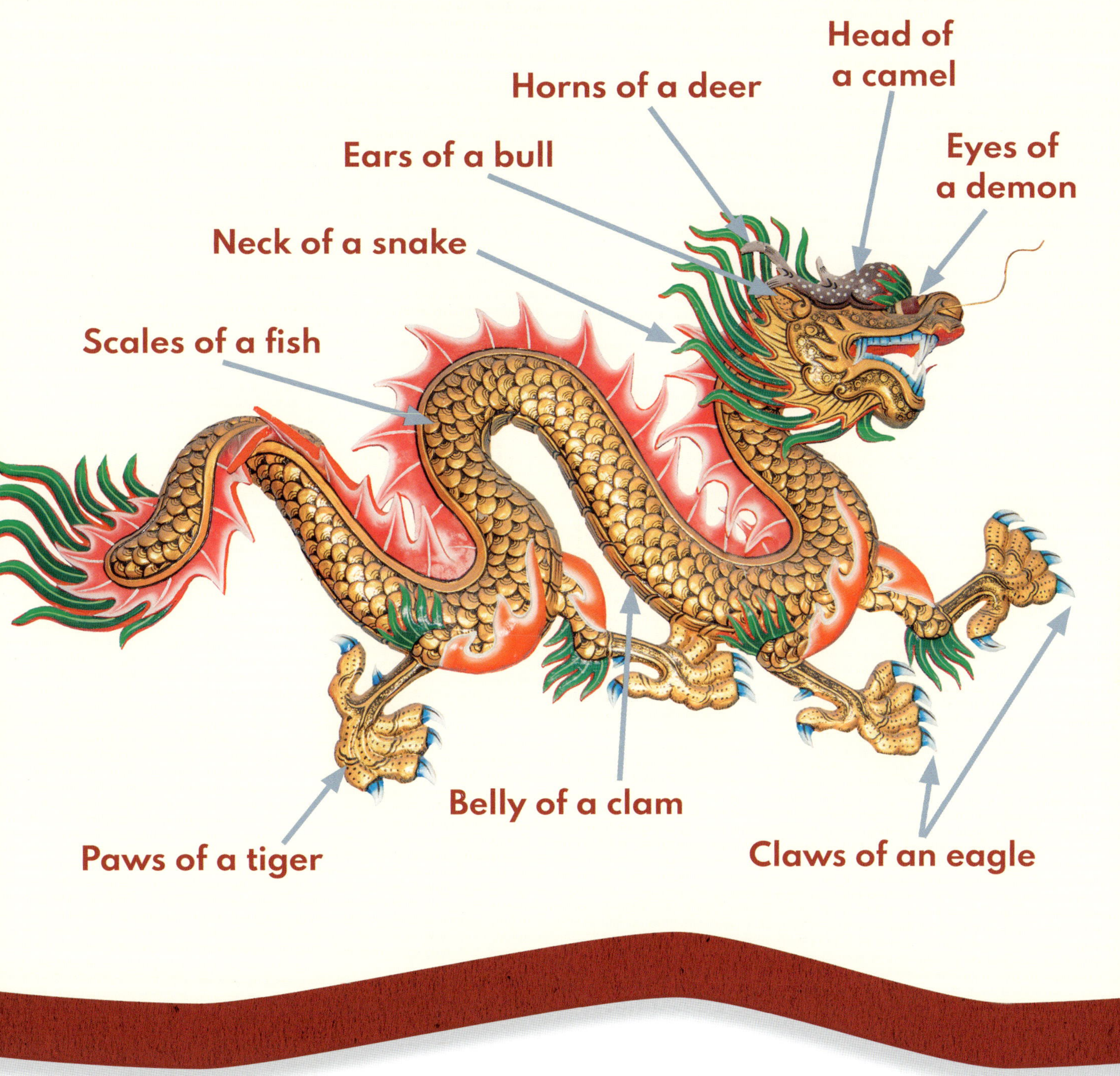

Dragons looked like a combination of many different creatures.

In Chinese culture, both dragons and bluebirds represent happiness.

A *feilong* is a type of dragon. One story describes them as having the head of a dragon, the tail of a **phoenix**, and colorful scales.

If someone accomplished great things, a feilong might appear. The person might even be allowed to ride on its back.

Dragons could take the form of an animal or person. They could grow as large as the universe. They could become as small as a **silkworm** or disappear altogether.

Bringing Good Things

Since good weather and rain help crops grow, farmers viewed dragons as sacred. Other people did too. For many, dragons are still a symbol of power and good fortune. They represent strength, protection, and happiness.

Dragons also represented the emperor. One myth told of an emperor who raised dragons.

The dragons would pull his chariot across the sky. The ruling emperor was known as "the dragon," and he sat on a dragon throne.

Fit for a King

Dragon robes were silk robes decorated with beautiful dragon motifs. The emperor's robe featured a dragon with five claws, a symbol of his power. The robes were worn during the Liao (901–1125), Ming (1368–1644), and Qing (1644–1911) dynasties.

Chinese scholar Lu Dian (1042–1102 CE) described why the dragon was so special:

> None of the animals is so wise as the dragon. His blessing power is not a false one. He can be smaller than small, bigger than big, higher than high, and lower than low.

Source: "Asian Dragons." *American Museum of Natural History*, n.d., amnh.org. Accessed 7 May 2022.

Comparing Texts:

Think about this quote. Does it support the information in this chapter? Or does it give a different perspective? Explain how in a few sentences.

Many Chinese people feel dragons are an important part of their culture.

CHAPTER 3

More than a Myth

Dragons are an important part of Chinese culture. They are so important that some people call themselves "**descendants** of the dragon." Many Chinese traditions and beliefs are based on myths about dragons.

The movement of the dragon dance is meant to portray the spirit of the dragon.

Dragons are some of the most popular images in Chinese art. They are often the subject of paintings and sculptures. Dragon designs are used on signs, flags, and clothes. People make life-size dragon puppets and kites to help celebrate traditional festivals.

Dragon dances are also held to celebrate special occasions. During this dance, a long, brightly colored dragon is held up with poles. Each pole is controlled by a different person. As they move, the dragon looks like it is moving. The dance was once a ceremony to help bring rain to an area. Today, it is a way to honor the dragon and bring good luck to the community.

Exciting races on the water are a highlight of the Dragon Boat Festival.

Celebrating on the Water

The Dragon Boat Festival celebrates dragons in another way. Dragon boats are long, narrow boats. They have a carved wooden dragon on

the front. People sit in pairs and row the boats with oars. They row to the beat of a drum.

Dragon Bone Cures

In traditional Chinese medicine, dragon bones were used to treat some sicknesses. The bones were actually fossils of animals. Some were even from dinosaurs. They were ground into a powder and mixed with herbs. Some people still use them today.

Chinese people honor and celebrate the role dragons play in their culture.

The Dragon Boat Festival honors the legend of Qu Yuan, a poet and court official. In 278 BCE, he jumped into the river to protest the actions of the new rulers of his state. Villagers rushed out in boats to rescue him, but it was too late. He had drowned. During the festival, people race dragon boats to remember his story.

Throughout the centuries, Chinese dragons have been important. They have been a symbol of good fortune, wisdom, and power. For many people, they are the symbol for Chinese culture itself.

Further Evidence

Look at the website below. Does it give any new evidence to support Chapter Three?

How Do You Do the Dragon Dance?

abdocorelibrary.com/dragons-of -chinese-mythology

LEGENDARY FACTS

To the Chinese people, dragons represent happiness and good luck.

Dragons are an important symbol of Chinese culture.

Dragons are an important part of many Chinese festivals and celebrations.

Glossary

descendants
people who come from a certain ancestor

herbs
plants used in medicine or to add flavor to food

motifs
decorative designs or patterns

phoenix
a mythological bird that dies in a fire but rises again from the ashes

prosperity
the state of being wealthy and successful

silkworm
an Asian moth caterpillar that makes silk thread to create its cocoon

Online Resources

To learn more about dragons of Chinese mythology, visit our free resource websites below.

Visit **abdocorelibrary.com** or scan this QR code for free Common Core resources for teachers and students, including vetted activities, multimedia, and booklinks, for deeper subject comprehension.

Visit **abdobooklinks.com** or scan this QR code for free additional online weblinks for further learning. These links are routinely monitored and updated to provide the most current information available.

Learn More

Gagliardi, Sue. *Mazu: Goddess of the Sea*. Abdo, 2023.

Krensky, Stephen. *The Book of Mythical Beasts & Magical Creatures*. DK, 2020.

Macfarlane, Tamara. *Dragon World*. DK, 2021.

Index

About the Author

Samantha S. Bell lives in the foothills of the Blue Ridge Mountains with her family and lots of cats. She is the author of more than 130 nonfiction books for kids.